Robertson

by John Mackay

LangSyne
PUBLISHING
WRITING *to* REMEMBER

Lang**Syne**

PUBLISHING

WRITING *to* REMEMBER

79 Main Street, Newtongrange,
Midlothian EH22 4NA
Tel: 0131 344 0414   Fax: 0845 075 6085
E-mail: info@lang-syne.co.uk
www.langsyneshop.co.uk

Design by Dorothy Meikle
Printed by Ricoh Print Scotland
© Lang Syne Publishers Ltd 2012

All rights reserved. No part of this publication may be reproduced, stored
or introduced into a retrieval system, or transmitted in any form or by any
means (electronic, mechanical, photocopying, recording or otherwise) without
the prior written permission of Lang Syne Publishers Ltd.

ISBN 978-1-85217-082-0

Robertson

SEPT NAMES INCLUDE:
Collier
Donachie
Duncan
Duncanson
Dunnachie
Inches
MacConachie
MacDonachie
Macinroy
MacLagan
MacRobb
MacRobert
MacRobie
Reid
Roy
Stark

Robertson

MOTTO:
Glory the Reward of Valour.

CREST:
A Right Hand holding an Imperial Crown.

PLANT BADGE:
Bracken.

TERRITORY:
From Rannoch Moor eastwards,
bounded on the north by Loch Rannoch
and the south by Glen Lyon.

Chapter one:

The origins of the clan system

by Rennie McOwan

The original Scottish clans of the Highlands and the great families of the Lowlands and Borders were gatherings of families, relatives, allies and neighbours for mutual protection against rivals or invaders.

Scotland experienced invasion from the Vikings, the Romans and English armies from the south. The Norman invasion of what is now England also had an influence on land-holding in Scotland. Some of these invaders stayed on and in time became 'Scottish'.

The word clan derives from the Gaelic language term 'clann', meaning children, and it was first used many centuries ago as communities were formed around tribal lands in glens and mountain fastnesses.

The format of clans changed over the centuries, but at its best the chief and his family held the land on behalf of all, like trustees, and the ordinary clansmen and women believed they had a blood relationship with the founder of their clan.

There were two way duties and obligations. An inadequate chief could be deposed and replaced by someone of greater ability.

Clan people had an immense pride in race. Their relationship with the chief was like adult children to a father and they had a real dignity.

The concept of clanship is very old and a more feudal notion of authority gradually crept in.

Pictland, for instance, was divided into seven principalities ruled by feudal leaders who were the strongest and most charismatic leaders of their particular groups.

By the sixth century the 'British' kingdoms of Strathclyde, Lothian and Celtic Dalriada (Argyll) had emerged and Scotland, as one nation, began to take shape in the time of King Kenneth MacAlpin.

Some chiefs claimed descent from

ancient kings which may not have been accurate in every case.

By the twelfth and thirteenth centuries the clans and families were more strongly brought under the central control of Scottish monarchs.

Lands were awarded and administered more and more under royal favour, yet the power of the area clan chiefs was still very great.

The long wars to ensure Scotland's independence against the expansionist ideas of English monarchs extended the influence of some clans and reduced the lands of others.

Those who supported Scotland's greatest king, Robert the Bruce, were awarded the territories of the families who had opposed his claim to the Scottish throne.

In the Scottish Borders country – the notorious Debatable Lands – the great families built up a ferocious reputation for providing warlike men accustomed to raiding into England and occasionally fighting one another.

Chiefs had the power to dispense justice

and to confiscate lands and clan warfare produced a society where martial virtues – courage, hardiness, tenacity – were greatly admired.

Gradually the relationship between the clans and the Crown became strained as Scottish monarchs became more orientated to life in the Lowlands and, on occasion, towards England.

The Highland clans spoke a different language, Gaelic, whereas the language of Lowland Scotland and the court was Scots and in more modern times, English.

Highlanders dressed differently, had different customs, and their wild mountain land sometimes seemed almost foreign to people living in the Lowlands.

It must be emphasised that Gaelic culture was very rich and story-telling, poetry, piping, the clarsach (harp) and other music all flourished and were greatly respected.

Highland culture was different from other parts of Scotland but it was not inferior or less sophisticated.

Central Government, whether in London

"The spirit of the clan means much to thousands of people"

or Edinburgh, sometimes saw the Gaelic clans as a challenge to their authority and some sent expeditions into the Highlands and west to crush the power of the Lords of the Isles.

Nevertheless, when the eighteenth century Jacobite Risings came along the cause of the Stuarts was mainly supported by Highland clans.

The word Jacobite comes from the Latin for James – Jacobus. The Jacobites wanted to restore the exiled Stuarts to the throne of Britain.

The monarchies of Scotland and England became one in 1603 when King James VI of Scotland (1st of England) gained the English throne after Queen Elizabeth died.

The Union of Parliaments of Scotland and England, the Treaty of Union, took place in 1707.

Some Highland clans, of course, and Lowland families opposed the Jacobites and supported the incoming Hanoverians.

After the Jacobite cause finally went down at Culloden in 1746 a kind of ethnic cleansing took place. The power of the chiefs was curtailed. Tartan and the pipes were banned in law.

Many emigrated, some because they wanted to, some because they were evicted by force. In addition, many Highlanders left for the cities of the south to seek work.

Many of the clan lands became home to sheep and deer shooting estates.

But the warlike traditions of the clans and the great Lowland and Border families lived on, with their descendants fighting bravely for freedom in two world wars.

Remember the men from whence you came, says the Gaelic proverb, and to that could be added the role of many heroic women.

The spirit of the clan, of having roots, whether Highland or Lowland, means much to thousands of people.

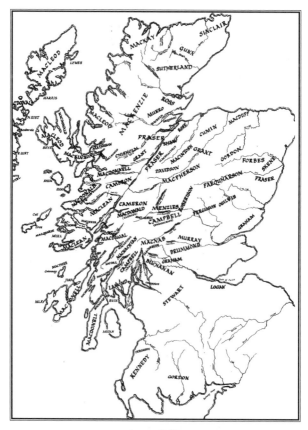

A map of the clans' homelands

Chapter two:

Picts and pirates

**Around the year 600 ad when the Picts domi-
nated the lands north of the valley of what
would be named the Forth and Clyde, monks
from religious houses in Ireland founded a
monastery at Dull in the north east end of
Loch Tay.**

These men of the Gaelic religion were the
ancestors of the Robertsons of Clan Donnachaidh.

As time went on, the monks were driven
from their monastery by the Picts but eventually
victoriously returned to Dull and took over the
abbey at Dunkeld where relics of St Columba had
been brought from Iona when that sacred isle
became a target for the Viking sea pirates.

It was a serious business guarding these
relics - and not only from the Vikings.

Fortunately in the Dark Ages monks
could transform themselves as occasion demand-
ed into part-time warriors when, led by a sword

wielding Abbot wearing a relic of Columba in defiance of the heathen enemy, they would give a good account of themselves.

Abbot Crinan was such a one, killed in action around the middle of the 11th century. He had held authority over the lands of Dull and Dunkeld. His wife Bethoc was a daughter of Malcolm II, King of both Scots and Picts, who, in battle against the warring Cumbrians and their southern allies, defeated them at Carham (between Coldstream and Kelso on the present Border line), driving them from their domination of the lands of Lothian as a result, thus initiating the forming of the Kingdom of Scotland.

Abbot Crinan's wife had given birth to a son who was christened Duncan.

He was heir to the throne but was slain by Macbeth who in turn was killed by Duncan's son Malcolm who became King Malcolm Canmore.

Succeeding families formed the Clan Donnachaidh (the latter name being Gaelic for Duncan) and the surname Robertson was taken by

Duncan who fought at Bannockburn after his men had rallied around their standard at St Ninians near Stirling. When the order to advance to the field of battle was given and the standard was pulled up from its temporary position, a strange gleam of light was reflected from the base of the hole in the earth. This light came from a crystal ball some two inches in diameter.

Such an unusual find in these superstitious, medieval times was thought to be of a magic significance and was taken by the chief into battle.

The resulting victory coinciding with this find may well have convinced the clan of its supposedly superior powers for it was carried into conflicts through ensuing years, whether in war or some brief foray, the arrangement of the varied hues coming from the rock crystal being studied avidly in the hope that omens would reveal the outcome of ensuing fights.

The crystal was first kept in a filigree gold holder then later in a silken pouch and now, as one of the clan treasures, is on view in the museum at Bruar.

Its healing properties have also been noted over the centuries.

In 1358 Robert of Atholl, who succeeded Duncan, married a daughter of Sir John Stirling of Glenesk in Angus whose lands in time passed to her nephew, Sir David Lindsay, a move disputed by Clan Donnachaidh.

When Lindsay arranged a tryst with Robert of Atholl's sons to peaceably discuss the matter, no sons appeared and, on a vassal of Lindsay's being sent to Atholl to enquire why, he never returned to Angus country to report; and this was followed by a foray eastwards into Angus lands by Donnachaidh warriors who slew more than 50 horsemen.

The 4th Chief's men also ravaged the church lands of Bishop Kennedy of St Andrews and Alexander Robertson, who succeeded as the 5th Chief, actually violated the Cathedral of Dunkeld by having his archers send flights of arrows into the worshippers during observation of the Mass.

On another occasion, Sir Robert Graham

and his henchmen murdered King James 1st in Perth. They were promoting the interests of the Earl of Atholl and the murderers fled into the remoter stretches of the Atholl lands but were hunted down by the fighting men of Donnachaidh and died by hideous torture in Edinburgh.

James II, as reward for the Chief's capture of "that most vile traitor, Robert the Graham", did in heraldic terms raise the Struan lands of Atholl into a Barony. This meant that, apart from various other privileges. the Chief could try wrongdoers in his own Baron's Court.

Chapter three:

Crossing swords

The 16th century, as far as the Clan Robertson was concerned, became an era of crossing swords with the governments of the day; and they treated the King's representatives with some contempt, as when James VI's two soldier guards arrived at a hostelry prior to arresting a local clansman for debt. They were unceremoniously hauled out of bed in the middle of the night and ejected from the house without even being given time to don their cavalry boots – if they could have found them, for they had disappeared as had their horses. A twenty mile hike back to their headquarters was the humiliating result.

The next century marked a different attitude to Royalty on the part of the Robertsons. In the 1630s, the rise of the Covenanters against Charles 1st, on his decreeing what manner they should worship, prompted the Robertsons to fight for their King.

They did this with bows and quivers of arrows, some guns, a pole axe, a few steel bonnets and one coat of mail: but, with the broadsword and targe and Highland bonnet still in the ascendant, their prowess earned them a mention in an old song with the lines 'Cam ye by Atholl, lad wi' the fillabeg, doon by the Tummel an' banks o' the Garry!'

The Marquis of Montrose raised Charles I's standard in Atholl, heralding a succession of Royalist victories and in 1650 the Athollmen led by the 12th Chief, Alexander, were fighting for his son Charles II - battling to oppose Cromwell, self-styled Lord Protector of Scotland.

Chapter four:

The great and the good

One famous member of the clan was William Robertson, born in the manse near Borthwick Castle in Midlothian in 1721 who had his early education in Dalkeith near Edinburgh, leaving school at 13 to become a student at Edinburgh University.

In his 14th year he had written into one of his books a Latin motto which expressed 'a love of literary fame' and this was to be realised sometime later.

He began his career in the ministry when he was 22, presiding over the congregation of Gladsmuir Kirk in East Lothian.

This is a good illustration of how, especially in the 18th century, one member of a clan could be a serious student in the world of books while his contemporary was leading

a Highland charge with the age-old savagery.

Fourteen years later, William Robertson produced his 'History of Scotland', his first important publication.

About this time, Robertson became joint pastor of Greyfriars Church in Edinburgh and a few years later was appointed chaplain of Stirling Castle, Moderator of the Church of Scotland, Principal of Edinburgh University and Historiographer Royal for Scotland.

His writings were appreciated abroad at a time when publishers must have surmounted problems of distribution for he was read in Continental countries and the Empress Catherine of Russia sent him a gold enamelled snuff box set with diamonds 'in admiring gratitude' for the pleasure and instruction she had been given by his histories.

Dr. William Robertson, as he was eventually titled, died in 1793 and his son, born in 1754, became a member of the Faculty of Advocates in his 21st year.

He is mentioned by the writer Lockhart as

'one of the most respected judges, Lord Robertson, who is the son of the great historian.'

In the Jacobite Rising of 1715 the Robertsons, Episcopalians or Presbyterians, were led by the 13th Chief Alexander Robertson of Struan (known as the Poet Chief) in support of the Catholic King James II whom they considered in the rightful line of monarchs although they did not share his religion.

The Chief led his men into battle carrying the charm stone previously mentioned (which was known in Gaelic as the 'Clach na Brataich' or 'Stone of the Standard').

A great flaw appeared in the stone prior to the battle of Sheriffmuir, a sign taken to predict the coming loss of Chieftainship power in the Highlands.

Neither side won the battle, though the Chief was captured: but only temporarily, being rescued by his militant sister 'Black Margaret' who, the year before, had 'borrowed' 50 clansmen from the Duke of Atholl in an attempt to claim her part of the moneys due to her by her brother but

was taken prisoner, escaped, was recaptured then spent some time chained up in a Dundee cell.

Old Struan - Chief Alexander - was destined for the church but had to leave his studies at St Andrews University to take over the responsibilities of leading the clan which did not join the '45 Rebellion as an organised group although the ageing chieftain mustered his tenants of Rannoch and the Braes of Atholl to prepare for the fight.

After the Jacobite victory of Prestonpans, Struan left Holyrood for home accompanied by a faithful retinue and in style, having acquired in the spoils of war the coach of the opposing commander, Sir John Cope.

On went the coach to Perthshire with Struan seated in Cope's place. When the vehicle came to wild country where no roads existed, it was hoisted on the broad shoulders of clan attendants to complete the journey to the Chief's home at Carie on the south side of Loch Rannoch.

The Chief had given over command of the Robertsons in the Prince's Highland army to his cousin Donald who was commissioned as a Lieutenant Colonel.

The old man died four years later. Two thousand mourners walked in the funeral procession the 18 miles from Carie to the burial place at Struan.

The estate was taken over by the government - his heir not being included in the pardon to other leaders who had taken part in the '45 Rising - but was restored in 1784 to Alexander Robertson of Struan, the 15th Chief.

If you like music, both military and classical, then you will like General John Reid, the son of Alexander Robertson of Straloch, whose ancestors were called Rua, meaning red, because the family was prone to ginger hair. The general did not sign himself Robertson but kept the name and signature of 'red' which he changed to Reid. He was an expert flute player and a great lover of music. He became a major in the 42nd Regiment (the Black Watch) and set the words of 'The Garb of Old Gaul' to music and it became the regimental march.

He left a large sum of money to establish a professorship at Edinburgh University where he had been a student. In his will he asked that on or about January 13th, the date of his birthday, an annual concert should be held in the hall of the professor of music and the programme should begin with one of his own composition and include 'The Garb of Old Gaul'.

The Reid concert tradition began and still continues and the audience always rises for 'The Garb of Old Gaul', the garb in question being the kilt.

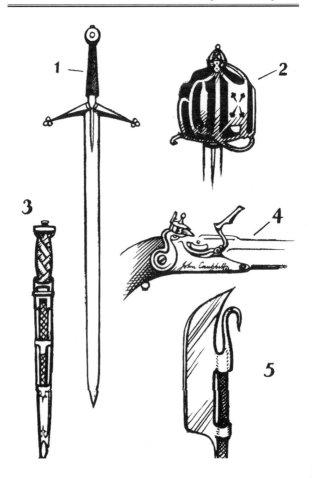

Highland weapons

1) The claymore or two-handed sword
   (fifteenth or early sixteenth century)

2) Basket hilt of broadsword
   made in Stirling, 1716

3) Highland dirk
   (eighteenth century)

4) Steel pistol *(detail)* made in Doune

5) Head of Lochaber Axe as carried
   in the '45 and earlier

GATHERING OF THE CLANS

CLAN MEMORABILIA FROM LANG SYNE

Books, postcards, Teddy bears, keyrings, mugs and much more...

Visit our website:
www.langsyneshop.co.uk

or write to us:
Lang Syne Publishing,
79 Main Street, Newtongrange,
Midlothian EH22 4NA
Tel: 0131 344 0414   Fax: 0845 075 6085
E-mail: info@lang-syne.co.uk